Garbage

Garbage

BY KAREN O'CONNOR

LUCENT
B·O·O·K·S

LUCENT *Overview Series* OUR ENDANGERED PLANET

LUCENT *Overview Series* OUR ENDANGERED PLANET

Library of Congress Cataloging-in-Publication Data

O'Connor, Karen, 1938-
  Garbage.

  (Lucent overview series)
  Bibliography: p.
  Includes index.
  Summary: Examines the dumping of garbage in oceans, on land, in the air, and in space and suggests possible solutions to this problem of waste pollution.
  1. Refuse and refuse disposal—Juvenile literature.
2. Pollution—Juvenile literature.   [1. Refuse and refuse disposal.
2. Pollution] I. Title. II. Series.
TD792.026 1989   363.72′8   89-9382
ISBN 1-56006-100-6

Contents

Introduction

Most of us toss our trash into a dumpster or stuff it down a garbage chute without much thought. We flush toilets, drain bathtubs, and grind up leftover food in a disposer with little concern about where the waste goes. We haul used furniture, old toys, worn-out bicycles, and battered car parts to the city dump unaware of what will happen to it next.

But we *all* need to pay closer attention to what we do with the waste, trash, litter, and garbage we produce each day. Did you know, for example, that every year garbage trucks in the United States collect about 133 million tons of solid waste? According to one report, a year's trash in New York City alone is enough to build a mile-high mountain in the middle of Yankee Stadium!

When we drop our trash on the street, toss it out a car window, or dump it into a lake or river, we pollute our cities, countryside, and waterways. When we explode rockets and leave leftover satellites in space, we trash the heavens.

When we burn garbage in our backyard or at a city dump, we foul the air. When we leave it out in the open, we spread disease. When we bury it, we risk having poisonous gases and liquids from the refuse seep into our drinking water. In the case of nuclear waste, discarded materials can take thousands of years to decompose.

Disposing of our waste, legally and illegally, has produced serious problems, especially in recent years when we throw away a large percentage of what we buy. From disposable dishes to disposable diapers, we've become known as a "throwaway" society.

What happens to this mountain of litter that reaches from the oceans to outer space? What happens to the millions of tons of hazardous toxic wastes produced annually? What happens to the thousands of pieces of broken satellites and chunks of exploded rockets that move through space? What happens to the tons of raw sewage that flow from our private and public bathrooms each year? And how do these waste products affect the quality of life on our planet?

There are no simple, straightforward answers. There may never be. We do know, however, that the problems are enormous and the need for a solution is urgent. People become ill from waste pollution. Many even die. Animal and plant life are threatened. Air and drinking water in many parts of the country are unsafe.

In some cities and towns across America, however, there are signs of hope as citizens, environmentalists, and government officials take action against waste pollution. Citizens of Cobb County, Georgia, for example, organized the Cobb Clean Commission, a volunteer litter cleanup project associated with a similar program called Keep America Beautiful.

Other groups, as well, are committed to recycling used products, managing landfills (garbage dumps) responsibly, and campaigning against litter. School students are working to restore neighborhoods and school grounds and are becoming aware of how their attitudes and behavior toward waste do make a difference.

Most people agree that waste management must continue to change and improve because our lives depend on responsible use of our natural resources. The earth is a closed system. The air and water we use today is the same air and water people have used throughout history. We cannot order new supplies from space!

CHAPTER ONE

New York's Gar-Barge

On March 22, 1987, a smelly sea vessel named *Mobro* sailed into history as it bobbed along the Atlantic Coast and into the Gulf of Mexico. The now-famous *gar-barge*, as it has been dubbed since, was loaded down with 3,168 tons of garbage, litter, waste, and trash from Islip, Long Island, and other New York townships.

Six thousand miles and 162 days later, the historic cruise ended back where it had begun, in New York Harbor. As the famous flat-bottomed boat pulled into the dock, it was still loaded down with the same 3,168 tons of garbage, litter, waste, and trash it had started with. Something funny, and serious, had happened along the way. Something that made headlines—and history.

How it all began

Months before the *Mobro* left port, New York State officials told Islip Township officials that their landfills—garbage dumps—were full. They could not be enlarged. Poisonous gases, disease from insects and rodents, and foul air from the garbage dumps were posing a serious health threat to citizens.

More garbage meant more problems. So Islip officials announced that they would accept residential trash only. Commercial businesses would have to find another place to dispose of their waste. Business owners were annoyed. The new decision could require hauling trash long distances by truck, sometimes to neighboring states miles away. The whole process would be expensive and time-consuming.

A good idea goes to waste

A man named Lowell Harrelson, the head of a construction company in Bay Minette, Alabama, heard about the situation in Islip. He came up with a plan—a good plan, he thought. Harrelson hoped to conduct an experiment in waste disposal that would show government officials and citizens that garbage can attract more than flies and swarming seagulls. He would turn this mound of garbage into a mountain of money.

First Harrelson spoke with Islip officials. They made an agreement that allowed Harrelson to take charge of the garbage. Next, he convinced the commissioners of Jones County, North Carolina, to allow him to deposit the trash on Radio Island, at the port of Morehead City. The idea was to let the garbage sit long enough to give off methane gas, a gas which builds up underneath garbage when organic matter decays without oxygen. Then they would extract the gas and sell it for a profit.

The chemical industry uses methane, which makes up a large part of natural gas, as a base material for many other chemicals.

After agreements with Islip and Jones County officials were complete, Harrelson put his plan into action. First he hired people to tie the trash into big bundles or bales, load it onto a barge, and then hitch the litter barge to the leased tugboat *Break of Dawn*.

Refuse refused

Next, Captain Duffy St. Pierre and his tugboat crew were given their orders. They were to haul the barge down the Atlantic Coast from New York to North Carolina, then deposit the bales of trash on Radio Island, as agreed. Everything happened according to plan—until they pulled into port at Morehead City. North Carolina officials had changed their minds. They were no longer willing to accept the bulging bales.

Stephen Reid of the state's Solid and Hazardous Waste Management Bureau said, ''We have enough garbage of our own. We don't need New York's.'' So the tugboat and barge pulled out of the North

Carolina port and continued down the coast in search of a place to unload the unwanted trash. But the search was not to end quickly or easily. What began as a simple experiment soon turned into an odyssey at sea that eventually attracted worldwide attention.

Mississippi officials said no to the litter barge, and so did officials from Alabama, Florida, Texas, and Louisiana. Some were more serious than others. Florida's governor Bob Martinez did not find the incident one bit funny. He had the power to shut out the teeming refuse, and he used it. All Florida ports were closed to the litter-laden *Mobro*.

Mobro, *New York's garbage barge, is hauled by the tug* Break of Dawn. *Loaded with 3,168 tons of New York garbage,* Mobro *seeks a place to dump its load. The barge has already been turned away by four states and two countries.*

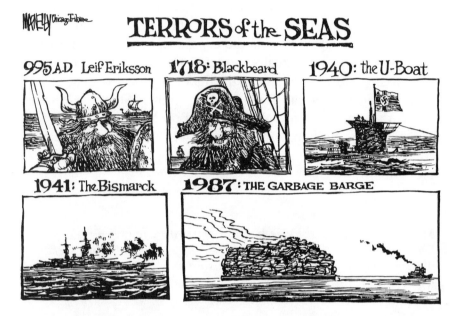

MACNELLY Chicago Tribune

TERRORS of the SEAS

995 A.D. Leif Eriksson   1718: Blackbeard   1940: the U-Boat

1941: The Bismarck   1987: THE GARBAGE BARGE

The governor of Louisiana, on the other hand, jokingly threatened to call out the National Guard if the captain and crew didn't get on their way. But as it turned out, he had good reason to refuse the refuse. When the weather-beaten barge pulled into the delta town of Venice, Louisiana's Department of Environmental Quality assigned inspectors to examine the festering bales.

Most of the contents were paper, but they also found syringes, bedpans, and other hospital items that could pose a health threat. Inspectors feared the oozing garbage and trash would leak into the river and pollute the water supply. So once more, the meandering *Mobro* was asked to sail on.

Next, Captain St. Pierre maneuvered the barge farther south. Perhaps a foreign country would be willing to take the unwanted trash. But alas, Mexico, the Bahamas, and tiny Belize in Central America closed their ports, as well. In fact, Belize took no chances. It even mobilized its small-plane Air Force against the barge of garbage.

Newspaper headlines soon proclaimed the bales of trash "the garbage without a country!"

Home sweet home

By early May the gar-barge had no choice but to head home. Islip officials did not exactly spread out a welcome mat. However, they did agree to let the barge unload at Islip—just this once—but only after the garbage had passed inspection at Long Island City and was taken by truck across Queens.

Citizens were not so sympathetic. Some Islip residents waved signs that read, "Ban the Barge!" And Claire Shulman, president of the borough of Queens, stopped the barge from docking in her borough by court order.

On May 16, the tugboat and barge pulled into New York Harbor. Within minutes Captain Duffy St. Pierre and his crew charged off the boat and up the ramp, tired, hungry, smelly, and almost desperate. They were interested in only two things—a good hot shower and a home-cooked meal! They had not been off the boat in over fifty days.

St. Pierre had meant business when he told reporters that he had planned to dock, no matter what. "I think they'll have to have gunboats to stop me," he said.

And that's exactly how New York City Mayor Ed Koch responded to their homecoming. Police Department launches with armed guards ordered the tug and barge to leave. Rejected once again, the *Mobro* and the *Break of Dawn* moved to Gravesend Bay, off Brooklyn, where they lay at anchor until further notice.

During the next three months, the *Mobro* became a popular tourist attraction, competing with such famous sites as the Empire State Building and the Statue of Liberty. Brooklyn residents lined the highways, peering at the famous tug and barge through telescopes. From the water, excursion boats and fancy yachts from nearby states circled the famous litter barge.

The *Mobro* gained television fame when Phil Donahue and Johnny Carson devoted time to the barge and its unexpected cruise to the Caribbean. Donahue stepped aboard the barge during one of his hour-long talk shows and hailed the bales as "the most famous three thousand tons of garbage in the history of the universe."

The bulging gar-barge, once an ordinary flat-bottomed boat, was fast becoming a national celebrity!

First-class burial

After the return of the *Mobro*, state and city officials struggled with where to put the trash and who should pay for it. Then on August 10, a state superior court judge in Brooklyn said the city could go ahead with its plan to burn the garbage. Judge Dominic Lodato said that Brooklyn officials and community groups had not proved that burning the trash and trucking the ash to the landfill on Long Island would be a health hazard or would violate state environmental laws.

Plans were made. Workers would dock the barge near the incinerator. There the city would build a ramp for unloading the bales, and then sanitation workers would break open the bundles to inspect them for infectious or hazardous materials. Next, the world-famous refuse would be burned in a Brooklyn incinerator. The four hundred tons of leftover ash would be buried at last in an Islip landfill—the very same landfill that originally turned it away!

On the morning of September 1, sanitation workers pulled on their protective suits and masks. Slowly they began snipping at the bulging bales. No one knew quite what to expect. The barge had roamed the ocean for months. All sorts of strange things could be lurking inside the soggy bundles.

After the last ties were snipped, the five inspectors stepped aside and watched a huge bulldozer break into the weather-beaten bundles. Paper and cardboard spilled out. Then plastic forks and spoons fell to the ground. Not much else was recognizable. Then suddenly, to everyone's surprise, out popped a huge family of—crickets—at least a million crickets who had come along for the ride!

That didn't discourage eager spectators or uniformed officials. The garbage barge was still a national celebrity, and people stood around in large numbers with great expectation to watch the ceremony. Vito Turo, New York's Sanitation Commission's chief spokesman, played it for all it was worth. He offered Garbage Barge '87 souvenirs— actual trash from the barge itself. Free! *Free* samples of a project that, by the time it was over, would have cost owner Harrelson and the state of New York more than one million dollars.

Loretta Smougasian, left, and Shirley Koch inspect garbage from Mobro. Special suits and masks protect them from hazardous fumes. After inspection, the trash will be burned.

Brendan Sexton, also from the Sanitation Commission, finally called a halt to all the fanfare. "I appreciate that this brought to people's attention that there is a waste disposal problem in America, but enough is enough. It's time to end it."

And what became of trash owner Lowell Harrelson and his waste disposal experiment? He told reporters he felt slightly depressed because he had hoped his idea would work out. "But I'm not completely turned off from the garbage business," he added. His experience with the gar-barge, Harrelson admitted, had helped him learn more about how people in business think and behave—information he expected would be useful in the future.

Cartoon or crisis?

The voyage of the *Mobro* was funny in many ways. But it was also serious because it pointed to one of the most pressing problems facing our nation today—waste management and disposal—or, simply, how and where to get rid of our garbage.

Alfred DelBello, former lieutenant governor of New York, sees the garbage odyssey as "a national embarrassment." He said that citizens could view it as material for a cartoon, or they can see it for what it is. "The people of the world watch America unable to cope with its most basic problem—its own waste," he said in an article for *American City and County*.

For citizens who are willing to look at the truth behind the odyssey of the garbage barge, there are many lessons. We can learn much about our resources and the way we use and often abuse them. *Or we can continue to deny the problem and go on disposing of our trash and garbage with little thought for the impact it will have on the quality of our lives.*

In Islip and hundreds of other United States towns, overcrowded landfills, plots of land set aside for dumping trash and garbage, are packed with mounds of decaying garbage that threaten underground water supplies.

Big cities such as New York, Detroit, Chicago, and Miami now burn part of their garbage, which saves the water but may pollute the air.

On the West Coast, Los Angeles County's Puente Hills landfill reaches its daily quota of twelve thousand tons of trash before noon. In Michigan's Dafter township, residents face a different problem. They are fighting in court to keep outsiders from using a private dump where eighteen dead buffaloes, oil sludge from a piston-ring factory, and sixty tons of trash a day from nearby Marquette are buried in a bulging mound that has already reached its limit.

New Jersey choking in garbage

New Jersey has one of the most serious conditions in the country. In May of 1987 Governor Thomas Kean signed a law passed by the state legislature requiring residents to separate reusable material from other refuse, so it can be recycled. This law could actually reduce by 25 percent the ten million tons of trash dumped each year into New Jersey's ten landfills. In January 1988 the state began exporting its garbage to neighboring states. ''Without further action,'' announced Governor Kean, ''New Jersey could actually choke on its own garbage.''

Half of the country's 18,500 landfills that were open ten years ago are now closed. Not only did they look bad and smell bad, but they also threatened air and water supplies. Some waste management officials report that by 1990, twenty-seven of the fifty states will have run out of landfill space.

There is much to be recycled among the 102 billion aluminum, glass, and plastic drink containers sold each year in America. It is also cheaper to recycle aluminum than to extract it from bauxite. Recycled paper can save trees. One report claims that to recycle one Sunday's edition of *The New York Times* would save seventy-five thousand trees.

Garbage dumps are also expensive to use and maintain. Philadelphia and Boston have run out of local landfills, and so they must haul their trash out of the area. In many cities hauling and disposal costs have quadrupled, ranging from ninety to 150 dollars per ton.

Incinerators, sometimes called trash burners, are one solution, but they create other problems. People don't want them in their neighborhoods because the gases and ash they produce could be toxic. And the ash doesn't just float away. It must be buried. This creates another space problem.

A crane lifts trash from a dumpster at a New York landfill. Half of America's 18,500 landfills that were open ten years ago are now filled to capacity with trash and garbage. Waste management officials predict that by 1990, more than half of the fifty states will have no land left for new landfills.

Newer incinerators that produce power when they burn trash and garbage are being manufactured. But they are costly—up to four hundred million dollars apiece. Burning trash that includes reusable items also wastes precious resources such as energy, metals, paper, and glass. For this reason, many states are creating mandatory recycling programs.

Plastic containers create a more serious disposal problem. Recyclers won't burn plastic because such burning produces high temperatures and corrosive gases.

Everyone's problem

According to a report in *Business Week*, the problem of waste removal on New York's Long Island is "urgent." Since most of the island rests on sensitive equipment that supplies drinking water, the state has decided to shut down all but one landfill by 1990.

Costs of waste removal in New York have gone from five dollars a ton three years ago to 150 dollars a ton today. Things will not change for the better until the town's 39-million-dollar resource recovery plant begins operating in 1990. In the meantime, the 300,000 citizens of Islip will have spent nearly 190 million dollars on waste disposal.

And New York is not alone in its trash problem. Forty-six of the fifty states are experiencing waste removal problems that range from serious to critical. "Garbage," as one headline phrased it, "isn't the other guy's problem anymore." The problem belongs to everyone.

CHAPTER TWO

A Tale of Three Cities

In December 1982, adults and children across the country prepared for Christmas. Carols rang out on radio and television. People hurried through shopping malls buying toys and gifts. Families and friends strung lights around the rooftops and decorated stately Christmas trees. There was a holiday feeling in the air in cities and towns everywhere. Everywhere—except Times Beach, Missouri.

Modern-day ghost town

In early December, citizens of this small community just southwest of St. Louis received some shocking news from the United States Environmental Protection Agency (EPA). The news not only ruined their Christmas celebration, but for many, it ruined their lives, as well.

Samples of soil revealed that the town had been drenched in dioxin, one of the most toxic (poisonous) chemicals known. Even one drop of dioxin in ten thousand gallons of liquid, or one part of dioxin per billion parts of soil, is considered highly hazardous.

The contamination had actually begun nine years earlier when local officials hired a man to spread oil on ten miles of unpaved streets in order to keep down the summer dust. They did not know at the time that the oilman's truck was also filled with sludge—soft, mudlike waste—from a chemical factory. The sludge contained the deadly dioxin. For at least two summers Russell Bliss oiled the streets of Times Beach. The contaminated oil was also spread throughout the state in about one hundred other locations. In the following months many people became ill, and small animals began dying unexpectedly, but no one knew why.

Over the next few years more people became ill and more animals died. Concerned citizens called for a federal investigation. Nine years later the EPA finally consented to test the soil. Results revealed the presence of dioxin.

On December 5, 1982, the Meramec River flooded the town and other nearby areas. Once again officials became alarmed. They feared that the loose soil which had washed into buildings and houses might be contaminated. They were especially concerned about the effect of the poison on household goods such as furniture and clothing.

EPA officials returned to Times Beach and checked the soil again. Tests showed that according to EPA standards, the flood-washed silt was free of contamination. Officials of the Centers for Disease Control in Atlanta, Georgia, however, warned residents to stay away from the town.

By Christmas most of the two thousand residents had moved elsewhere temporarily. Then in February 1983, the EPA suddenly offered to buy the entire town. It was the first such offer in the history of this government agency. The purchase offer also included moving residents to a safer area upriver—a move which ultimately cost the EPA thirty-three million dollars.

Within months Times Beach, Missouri, became a ghost town. Weeds and tall grass huddled around abandoned houses and empty shops. A few cars remained behind, along with a bird feeder made from an old plastic bottle and a hammock suspended between two trees. A friendly sign that read THANKS FOR COMING stood in front of the Easy Living Laundromat. And at Easy Living Mobile Manor, a few trailers stood deserted. Today there are no people left in Times Beach. Easy living became impossible living in this once-cozy river town.

Medical researchers are unsure of the exact effects of dioxin exposure to human life over a ten-year period. Cancer and birth defects are among the worst fears. Former residents of Times Beach, however, know firsthand what the deadly poison has done to friends and family and pets.

Most remember the dead birds and the stillborn kittens and puppies. Some recall neighbors who died of cancer and childbirth. Marilyn Leistner, the town's last mayor, drove one reporter through town, indicating one tragedy after another that had resulted from exposure to the toxic waste.

Nearly every house she pointed to held the memory of some friend or relative who had died. ''Kidney cancer over there,'' she said, pointing to one house, ''and this next family, the dog had a seizure disorder, and their little girl had terrible stomach and bladder problems.''

Warning sign blocks the entrance to Times Beach, Missouri. Danger from dioxin contamination forced town officials to evacuate residents and seal off the town. The EPA relocated residents at a cost of 33 million dollars.

The mayor also had her own story to tell. One grown daughter almost died of cancer, another tried to commit suicide, and her ex-husband had a problem with his liver.

Former resident Michael Reid remembered that as a child, he and his friends had loved to ride their bikes behind the oil truck, skidding and sliding in the slippery goo. Penny Capstick recalled falling down in the stuff, and a little girl named Jeri Lynn used to sit by the side of the road and kick her feet in it.

Also hard to take was the way outsiders treated Times Beach residents once they heard about the eerie waste. "When you say Times Beach to people," says Leistner, "they look you up and down to see if you're green or glow in the dark." "If you lived in Times Beach," added Rose Eisen, "you're the scuzz of the earth."

Two EPA technicians test mounds of debris for dioxin at Times Beach, Missouri. A flood caused contaminated soil to wash into buildings and houses. Dioxin is so toxic that one drop in 10,000 gallons of liquid is considered hazardous.

Former residents miss their town and the good times they enjoyed. "Down in the Beach," said Joe Capstick, "everybody knew everybody's business. Up here," he continued, talking about their new life in Hilltop Village, "it's a totally different lifestyle. They barely say hi. Back in Times Beach you could go down at ten in the morning and find half the town fishing. It was fun."

Today, however, the former residents of Times Beach have only their memories and photographs to remind them of the life they once had in this small midwestern town on Interstate 44 in Missouri.

Holbrook, Massachusetts—toxic playground

The Pastures had been a favorite play spot for children of Holbrook, Massachusetts, "for ages and ages," as one mother recalled. It was almost as though this plot of vacant land belonged to the young. It was ideal for a neighborhood game of hide-and-seek, building a secret fort, daredevil biking over the Camel Humps, or just a time of quiet reading.

The Pastures also held a kind of science-fiction fascination for many of the young local residents. A strange jellylike goo referred to as "green slime" or "moon glob" provided them with hours of fun hurling handfuls of the gunk at each other like snowballs.

There were also plenty of empty industrial barrels—perfectly suited to a joyride downhill. The Pastures was a kid's paradise. Even parents stayed away—until 1982 when the EPA placed this land near the top of its national list of high-priority hazardous waste sites.

Until then residents had no idea that the empty barrels and the green gunk that provided their children with so many hours of fun were as lethal as a loaded gun. They did not know enough about the hazards of waste from poisonous chemicals to realize that these deadly playthings had come from the Baird & McGuire pesticide manufacturing plant located at the edge of The Pastures.

The events that took place were similar to those in Times Beach and other stricken cities. Between 1979 and 1983, according to the Massachusetts Department of Public Health, twenty-four men from

Holbrook died of lung cancer. Others during the same period were dying of bladder cancer at three times the average rate. And more than twice the average number of women from Holbrook died of cancer of the female organs.

Despite the high rates of death and health problems, however, many residents refused to get involved in the fight to clean up their town. But others did enough to make up for the many who did nothing. Joanne O'Donnell was one of these.

All five of her now-grown children had played at The Pastures when they were young. Four of them wound up with endocrine (gland) problems. One daughter had a tumor on her pituitary gland. Another had her spleen removed in 1984.

As a boy, O'Donnell's eldest son Mark had been known for his feisty moon-glob fights and his thundering downhill rides in the big metal drums. He even worked at the nearby pesticide factory one summer while in high school. Then years later at age twenty-seven, Mark came down with ''some crazy pneumonia that nobody could figure out,'' O'Donnell said.

Which of these mammals is more intelligent?

Esther Ross, a resident of nearby Randolph, Massachusetts, says she became worried in 1981 when she realized she was attending a lot of funerals. "The people next door," she told a reporter, "were stricken by cancer, and the people next door to them and next door to them. We had a six-year-old pass away from cancer in the neighborhood and a twenty-year-old."

Together O'Donnell, Ross, and Leah Abbott formed a group called People United to Restore the Environment. One day while the pesticide factory was still operating, Abbott marched right into president Baird's office and asked to see the poisonous chemicals firsthand.

In 1983 town officials forced the plant to close. But that was not the end of the scare. Frightening bulletins and warnings continued. The EPA found more toxic wastes from deadly chemicals such as arsenic, DDT, and chlordane in the soil and water around the factory. Greatest was the danger to the drinking water. Three of the town's wells were located next to Baird & McGuire.

Early in 1985 chemical waste was found leaking into the nearby Cochato River. And in later tests the river's sediment also produced traces of poisonous waste from arsenic and another deadly chemical, naphthalene. During the summer of 1985 the EPA became even more alarmed when they discovered concentrations of dioxin at the pesticide factory.

Abbott organized a public meeting in 1985 at Holbrook High School. There EPA officials faced three hundred angry residents who demanded to know why, after three long years, Baird & McGuire still had not been cleaned up. Soon after the meeting, the EPA agreed to all of the group's demands. In August, workers erected a new chain link fence with a barbed wire top, and installed warning signs around the pesticide plant.

Many residents of Holbrook, including those who had worked so hard on the cleanup campaign, decided to continue living in the town. "Where am I going to move that it's not going to crop up in my backyard again?" Leah Abbott responded to a visiting reporter. "Where is safe?"

Disaster on the Nevada desert

Jacqueline Saunders was only five years old in 1951, but she clearly remembers that time in her life. She and her family often sat on the steps of their home in St. George, Utah, to watch pastel-colored clouds rise above the nuclear test site in the nearby Nevada desert.

Between 1951 and 1962 the Atomic Energy Commission (AEC), an agency of the United States government, exploded one hundred weapons on this desert site, selected because of its remote location and small population. Following an explosion, waste material falls to the ground in the form of radioactive particles or dust. Nuclear fallout, as it is sometimes called, is highly dangerous.

Army observers watch atomic blast on Yucca Flat near Las Vegas, Nevada. Following the explosion, radioactive particles fell to the ground. These particles, called "nuclear fallout," have been blamed for causing cancer and other illnesses.

"The government assured us there would be no danger," Saunders told reporters. But Jacqueline Saunders, along with hundreds of other residents of St. George and surrounding communities who were exposed to the nuclear fallout, developed cancer and other illnesses in later years.

In May 1984 Judge Bruce Jenkins, a United States district court judge in Salt Lake City, Utah, ruled that the federal government was responsible for these resulting health problems. He claimed the government had not adequately warned residents, especially those who lived downwind of the Nevada test site, of the physical dangers from nuclear fallout.

As a result, Jacqueline Saunders and the families of nine other victims—now dead—were awarded 2.6 million dollars in a lawsuit they had filed against the United States government. But the government has denied being negligent, and the case may have to go all the way to the United States Supreme Court before the matter is settled.

To most of the residents involved in the case, money was not the important issue. The lawsuit was meant to draw attention to the situation, and to press for stricter safety standards in the future development and testing of nuclear weapons.

Isaac Nelson, for example, knows the settlement cannot bring back his wife, who died of a brain tumor that may have resulted from exposure to radiation. "Some people think we have won a lot," Nelson told a reporter, "but I don't have any more respect for it than if we had won the first leg in a long relay race."

Claudia Peterson appears to feel the same way. "My faith in many things has been badly shaken," she said in an article in the January 1987 issue of *Redbook* magazine. "What has happened is incredible to me."

Like Jacqueline Saunders, Peterson grew up in St. George, Utah, near the atomic bomb site, and people close to her also have been affected by nuclear fallout.

"Many of our friends and neighbors have some form of cancer, or their relatives have died from it,'' she said. The town also has an unusually high number of retarded children, born during the years of heaviest testing.

Peterson's six-year-old daughter Bethany has stage four neuroblastoma, a cancer of the nervous system that also involves the bones and bone marrow. Her sister Cathy has had cancer of the lymph nodes.

Peterson remembers that when she was a child, exploding bombs colored the sky with billowy pink and orange clouds, then dumped grayish-white ash all over the cars and streets and vegetable gardens. In the nearby town of Mesquite, kids at play filled their pockets and their mouths with this ashen ''snow.''

Everyone knew about the testing because the government had asked residents to cooperate while the explosions took place. Officials told

Citizens gather to watch atomic blast near Las Vegas, Nevada. Though most observers are wearing protective goggles, many are forced to shield their eyes from the brilliant flash. These observers are seven miles from the blast.

them that radiation fallout could be harmful, could even cause death in large doses, but that the level they would be exposed to would be no worse than that of dental X-rays.

The people believed what they were told. Some families even packed a picnic lunch and sat on their lawns to watch the spectacular show! They believed that in their own way, they were contributing to the security of their country by supporting the national defense program. Peterson's parents, however, in 1953 first became seriously concerned about the testing. That summer, following a series of explosions in mid-May, nearly one-quarter of all the sheep in Nevada and Utah mysteriously died.

Nuclear fallout creates misery

Local ranchers filed suit against the government in 1955 for the loss of more than seventeen thousand sheep, but officials insisted that the deaths were not related to the testing. ''No one could believe that the government would harm us intentionally,'' said Peterson, although some people did wonder if even the government really knew the potential for long-range harm.

Now the Petersons and others do know—from personal experience—the tragic effects of the nuclear fallout. Several of their friends have cancer. Three have children with leukemia. Prior to the testing, cancer rates had been lower than the national average in this Mormon community. Between 1957 and 1974, however, cases of acute leukemia rose to one and one-half times the national average. The statistics for other cancers are also higher than the norm.

Peterson's daughter Bethany is being treated at a government-funded children's hospital in Salt Lake City. ''The doctors there refuse to say whether radioactive fallout is the cause of her illness,'' said Peterson. ''But I'm convinced that the testing made Bethany sick.''

The Petersons are aware that some of their neighbors have sued the government, but they are reluctant to take that action themselves. ''The worst part,'' Claudia Peterson added, ''is that the testing still has not stopped. It has only moved underground.'' Since 1980 at least fifteen bombs—some a hundred times more powerful than the bomb dropped on Hiroshima—have been exploded each year.

People ask the Petersons why they don't move. They don't move, said Claudia Peterson, because southern Utah is their home, and moving would mean leaving the people and things they love. "Besides, leaving wouldn't guarantee that we would be spared the effects of radiation," she said. "The damage has already been done. The best thing I can do now is try to help cancer victims in our community."

No one is safe

None of us is completely safe from the effects of hazardous chemical and nuclear waste, because the problem of how to dispose of it safely is still not solved.

In fact, it appears that we are creating toxic waste more rapidly than we can ever dispose of it. In 1982 a survey conducted by the Environmental Protection Agency estimated that 115 billion pounds of toxic hazardous wastes are created each year as manufacturing by-products. By 1990 the volume will grow to 176 billion pounds.

The hazards of nuclear wastes are even more sobering. As nuclear power production increases, high-level radioactive nuclear waste also increases. These wastes remain dangerously radioactive for thousands of years. They contain plutonium, which has been proven to cause cancer, birth defects, and other fatal conditions in human beings.

CHAPTER THREE

Tidal Wave of Plastic

A young sea turtle, undernourished and unable to dive for food, was found on a beach in Hawaii. It died two days later. George Balazs, a sea turtle biologist with the National Marine Fisheries Service, dissected the turtle to discover the cause of death.

He found a plastic food storage bag filled with garbage, some pieces of pumice stone, a plastic golf tee, shreds of bag sheeting, bits and pieces of plastic fishing line, a plastic flower, part of a bottle cap, a comb, chips of Styrofoam, and dozens of small round pieces of plastic.

"The intestine was completely blocked with this stuff," reported Balazs.

Plastic poison

Ocean pollution affects everyone. Garbage dumped at sea fouls the water, washes ashore and litters our beaches, and creates sights and smells that spoil the natural beauty of planet earth. And one of the most destructive aspects of ocean pollution is plastic trash and its effect on one of earth's most precious resources—marine wildlife.

Plastic debris is a deadly threat to birds, ocean mammals, fish, and other sea creatures. Every day, marine plants and animals die by nibbling on, swallowing, or becoming entangled in one or more of the five million pieces of plastic trash dumped into our oceans each day. This trash includes Styrofoam drinking cups, six-pack rings, packaging pellets, trash bags, and some fifty thousand tons of lost or discarded plastic fishing nets.

Death nets

For millions of marine animals, plastic fishing nets are more deadly than any other form of plastic trash. Years ago fishing nets were made of material, usually hemp or flax, that would eventually disintegrate. But today's sturdy plastic nets are nearly indestructible. In the North Pacific, according to one report, netting pulled from the sea held captive one hundred dead seabirds and two hundred dead salmon entangled in a *single* piece.

In 1986 the Center for Environmental Education (CEE), with help from the Fish and Wildlife Foundation, began to compile a report of all the known incidents in North America of marine wildlife becoming tangled in commercial and recreational fishing nets.

According to Kathy O'Hara of CEE, the report includes animals that are entangled in lost or discarded fishing gear and other plastic debris, as well as swallowing of plastics by wildlife. This report was distributed to scientists, government officials, and fishing industry officials to encourage them to discuss the various laws and policies that would protect marine wildlife. The report helped gain support for the Marine Mammal Protection Act, which was reauthorized in 1988.

This study, and the regulations that result, are of the greatest importance because many of the captive marine creatures, such as humpback, fin, and right whales, are on the endangered species list. From 1978-1986, according to the CEE report, observers saw 215 marine mammals caught in nets belonging to foreign vessels. Common dolphins and pilot whales made up 93 percent of the total.

Since 1975 a total of twenty-six cetaceans (fishlike marine mammals) became entangled in buoy lines of lobster traps. Twenty of them were endangered whales.

During a ten-year period, more than thirty endangered West Indian manatees, which search for food in shallow coastal waters, were found entangled in nets along the coast of Florida. Several died.

In 1985, 333.7 million pounds of shrimp at a value of 472.8 million dollars were caught in the southeast Atlantic and Gulf of Mexico.

But in the process, thousands of sea turtles were also caught and drowned in trawl nets meant for the shrimp. Most of them were very young loggerhead turtles.

California's gill nets do some of the worst damage in the industry. Gill nets are fishing nets with mesh that is big enough to allow the head of a fish to pass through but that entangles the fish when it tries to withdraw. Each year, a minimum of 100 sea otters, 1,000 California sea lions, 100 harbor seals, and possibly up to 25 elephant seals, 30 pilot whales and an unknown number of gray, humpback, and finback whales are caught incidentally in gill nets.

In Alaska, harbor seals and sea lions, sea otters, humpback and gray whales, and porpoises, as well as some eight hundred seabirds, also drown yearly in gill nets.

These nets are so harmful to seabirds and marine mammals that regulations are under way to restrict their use in areas heavily populated by these species. In addition, the National Oceanic and Atmospheric Administration (NOAA) has set up a special office in Seattle, Washington, directed by James M. Coe, called the Marine Entanglement Program.

A seal with a plastic ring around his muzzle lies dead on the beach. Unable to open his mouth to eat, the seal probably starved to death. Sea animals, drawn by curiosity to investigate plastic items thrown onto beaches, often become entangled and die.

Recreational fishing is also responsible for the entanglement and death of several endangered species including brown pelicans, manatees, and several species of sea turtles. According to the CEE report, ''One leatherback turtle found in New York had actually ingested [swallowed] 590 feet of heavy duty monofilament fishing line.''

Slow death

But entanglement is not the only cause of slow death for millions of sea creatures each year. There are others, and, like the fishing nets, they too are made of plastic.

In Texas, two loggerhead sea turtles were discovered stranded on the beach, one with a piece of a plastic onion sack around its neck. Other turtles have ingested plastic bags, pieces of plastic bottles, and even a plastic milk carton.

A sea turtle survives near-strangulation by a fishing net. Many marine animals, including endangered species, become trapped and die in fishing nets, fishing lines, and other debris each year. Certain types of nets are so harmful that laws are being considered to restrict their use.

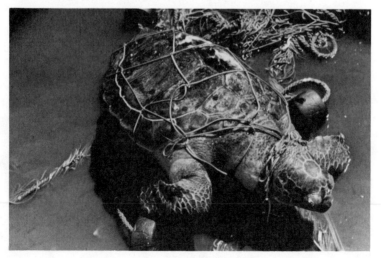

Plastic pellets fill a bird's stomach. Plastic pellets are the raw form of plastic that is melted down and molded into plastic bottles and other objects. Adult birds not only feed on plastic pellets, but they also bring them home to feed their chicks.

A study of albatross chicks by the United States Fish and Wildlife Service found that 90 percent of the birds had at least some quantity of plastics in their digestive tracts.

Marine mammals are also threatened by ocean garbage. On New Year's Day in 1984 an infant pygmy sperm whale was found stranded beside his dying mother on a Galveston beach. Scientists tried to restore him in a local aquarium, but one day he died suddenly. An autopsy (examination of the dead body) revealed that the young whale had swallowed a large plastic bag, a bread wrapper, and a corn chip bag. The plastic had blocked his digestive tract, and he died of starvation.

Befouled beaches

Plastic trash not only pollutes the deep sea as well as coastal waters, but also affects our recreational beaches, turning them into a sandscape of plastic pop bottles, plastic drinking cups, plastic lunch bags, and plastic sand toys.

To Anthony Amos, a University of Texas oceanographer, collecting plastic and other beach trash is all in a day's work. Several times a week over the past five years, Amos has inspected the 7½-mile

Amount of Trash Dumped Annually into the World's Oceans

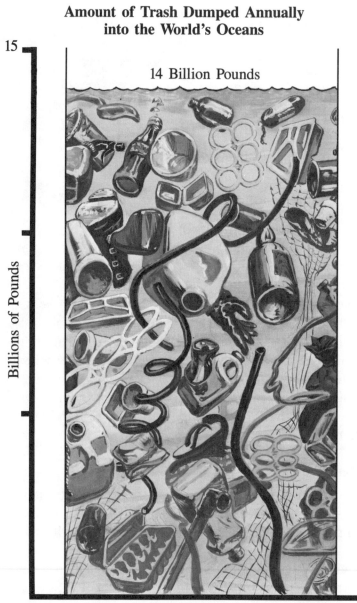

15

Billions of Pounds

14 Billion Pounds

Trash

coast of Mustang Island, south of Galveston, Texas. Paint cans, plastic mop handles, disposable plastic lighters, Christmas tree lights, clumps of disintegrating plastic cups, and bottles of toilet-bowl cleaners from around the world are just some of the thousands of pieces of garbage that wash ashore there each year.

Galveston is a busy international seaport, so it may not be too surprising to discover trash fouling public beaches. But the problem doesn't stop there. Even the most remote beaches are no longer sheltered from the sights and sounds and smells of man-made waste—plastic and otherwise.

Walk along the coastline of Washington's Olympic National Park and you'll stumble over bottles from Japan. Tour one of the tiny western island beaches of Hawaii, two thousand miles from the coast of California, and you will be immediately reminded of life on the mainland. Scraps of rope, plastic fishing lines and nets, and plastic containers are among the collection that has washed ashore there.

Oregon residents discovered for themselves how weighty the problem is. Those who participated in a coastal cleanup walk in 1984

A plastic six-pack ring claims the life of a fish. Because plastic is not biodegradable, this six-pack ring will still be around hundreds of years from now.

picked up twenty-six *tons* of trash in just three hours. Among their pickings were plastic fishing gear, plastic sandals, plastic lunch bags, and plastic packaging pellets.

Ocean dump

Litter and garbage from ships are partly to blame for the state of our beaches. The National Academy of Sciences estimates that almost a million pounds of plastic trash are dumped into the oceans every day. During the 1970s an international treaty, MARPOL (Marine Pollution Convention), and the Ocean Dumping Act were drafted in order to ban dumping trash overboard.

MARPOL's regulation against dumping *plastic*, however, was covered in an optional section called Annex V. This meant that the part of the treaty covering plastics could not be enforced until more countries signed it. Therefore, it had little effect for over ten years.

Then in late 1987, a new wave of interest in the treaty swelled as the Reagan administration and sea-related organizations urged approval of the Annex. On December 29, President Reagan signed Annex V of the MARPOL treaty, which prohibits the disposal of plastic garbage from ships anywhere in the sea, and prohibits the disposal of all garbage within twelve miles of the shore.

In addition, the new legislation requires NOAA to continue to identify the deadly effects of plastics on the marine environment. It also requires the EPA to identify sources on land that create plastic and other types of pollution and report on ways to reduce them.

The Gulf states office of the Center for Environmental Education (CEE) is involved in related work. This agency keeps track of beach garbage by category, and from time to time officials come across an item that requires a new classification. In 1987 the CEE had to add a new classification for an item that had suddenly begun turning up along the south coast of Texas in 1986—plastic-covered disposable diapers!

Interest in plastics arose during the mid 1940s, following World War II. Materials that were both disposable and durable appealed to manufacturers as well as the buying public. By the 1960s plastic was in wide use for everything from commercial fishing gear to oxygen-barrier bottles that can keep the fizz in soft drinks.

Over the next twenty years, the plastics industry refined its products to the point where, today, plastic food containers can go from the freezer to the microwave oven to the kitchen table to the garbage can in a matter of minutes!

This may be good news for hungry students, busy professionals, single parents, and the elderly who live alone, but it's a mountain of bad news for scientists and researchers whose job it is to keep our land, sea, and sky clean and safe.

Some states have begun attacking the problem at the source. Government officials are encouraging scientists and manufacturers to create biodegradable plastics—plastics that can break down into harmless components.

By the fall of 1986, eight states were requiring that plastic six-pack rings be made of biodegradable materials. Twenty-four other states were taking similar action. These new plastics remain sturdy while in stores or houses, but decompose when exposed to the sun's ultraviolet rays.

Since ultraviolet rays do not penetrate the ocean, however, scientists will have to come up with a different formula for plastics used at sea. Perhaps they can create a plastic that will decompose in saltwater.

But for now, disposing of plastic and other toxic wastes can be dangerous. It is certainly more complicated than getting rid of every-day garbage. As a result, some states require residents to separate plastic and toxic waste products from ordinary household trash before disposing of it.

Engineers and scientists are also at work designing and constructing a variety of furnaces that can break down the toxic molecules in plastic into safer compounds without producing dangerous by-products such as dioxin.

CHAPTER FOUR

Extraterrestrial Trash

In June, 1983, on the third day of the STS-7 orbital mission, Commander Robert Crippen noticed a pit—a small hole—on the outside of one of the *Challenger*'s windows. He reported the damage to mission control. After the orbiter landed, workers inspected the pit and replaced the damaged window with a new one. Next they removed the pitted piece of glass and sent it to the National Aeronautics and Space Administration's (NASA) Johnson Space Center (JSC) in Houston, Texas. There scientist Dave McKay and others used a specially equipped electron microscope to scan the pitted glass.

Fused into the window was a particle containing chemicals such as carbon, aluminum, potassium, and other ingredients that make up white paint. Findings showed the particle had traveled between 1.86 and 3.1 miles per second and measured about .0078 inches in diameter.

From this information, they concluded that while in orbit, the STS-7 *Challenger* had collided with a piece of space debris—a flake of paint! Imagine a tiny flake of paint creating a hole large enough to damage a window that was five-eighths of an inch thick, built to withstand eighty-six hundred pounds of pressure per square inch, and resist temperatures of 482 degrees centigrade (900 degrees Fahrenheit)!

Yet that is exactly what happened. And the energy from the impact of this postage stamp-sized paint flake against the window was equal to that of a bowling ball going sixty miles per hour.

Several months after the *Challenger* incident, Soviet engineers reported a similar impact to one of the windows of their *Salyut 7* spacecraft. In this case, the crew reported actually hearing the impact.

Scientists believe that as spacecraft expand and contract as a result of becoming hot and then cold, the surface paint may slowly begin to flake off. These orbiting flakes are then classified as space debris.

Because objects in orbit travel at amazingly fast speeds, some as much as twenty-five thousand feet per second, even tiny specks of debris can cause great damage when they collide with a large object. A particle of debris not much bigger than a grain of salt, for example, can puncture a hole in a spacesuit large enough to force an astronaut to return to the spacecraft immediately or risk death from loss of pressure.

From baseballs to marbles

Paint flakes are just one type of extraterrestrial (outer space) trash. Old satellites, chunks of exploded rockets, nose cones, sometimes called "space junk," and millions of smaller pieces of debris are also trashing the universe. Radars monitored by the North American Aerospace Defense Command (NORAD) now track more than five thousand objects larger than the size of a baseball.

"There are probably more like forty thousand smaller bits, marble size and larger," claims NASA space debris expert, Donald J. Kessler, "billions of paint flakes, and tens to hundreds of trillions of still smaller dust-sized particles that have not been detected since NORAD's radar simply cannot keep track of everything."

Other major types of space debris include exploded United States and Soviet rocket bodies. "A spacecraft can be blown into as many as two hundred trackable fragments," said Kessler, "but we know from ground tests that a thousand or more pieces slightly larger than a centimeter, or less than half an inch, can also appear."

Leftover fuel and oxygen in these rockets' fuel tanks will eventually react and cause explosions sending bits of debris into orbit.

Specks represent man-made objects orbiting the earth. The smallest objects are 10 centimeters (about 4 inches) in diameter. Objects in orbit can travel as fast as 25,000 feet per second.

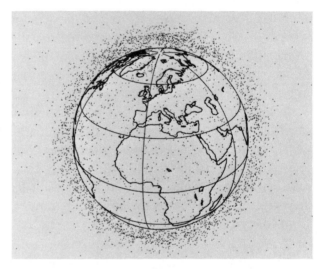

The United States now prevents such explosions by burning off the excess fuel in the tanks after the rockets have completed their missions.

The few fragments that can be seen do not pose much of a threat to spacecraft because they can be tracked by radar and telescopes and then avoided. The smaller pieces of debris, however, are more hazardous than they might seem, considering their size, because they are "hidden" by the vastness of space.

Breakthrough!

"The first real proof that man-made orbital debris was striking spacecraft was the S-149 particle collection experiment aboard Skylab," said Kessler. At the end of the Skylab program in 1974, the windows on a returned Apollo Command Module were inspected by a scanning electron microscope. Scientists on the project discovered that about one-half of the pits covering the windows were lined with aluminum, probably caused by collisions with aluminum oxide particles from solid rocket motor exhaust.

Currently 460 waste fragments from a nine-month-old third stage booster are being tracked. Through this study and others, scientists hope to learn enough about space debris to help them develop a collision warning system for the space station that is scheduled for launch in the early 1990s.

The one-billion-dollar Hubble Space Telescope scheduled for launch is also of concern to scientists. Its projected life is seventeen years, but researchers say it may not survive to carry out a full mission.

Michael Shara, an assistant astronomer at the Space Telescope Science Institute in Greenbelt, Maryland, claims, "There is roughly a one percent chance of it being destroyed by debris during its lifetime." A collision with a ten-centimeter (3.9-inch) or larger object would probably destroy the telescope.

Protective devices

Scientists are continually researching ways to protect spacecraft from colliding with debris. One method involves the installation of an aluminum "bumper" or outer sheet, separated from the wall of the shuttle. Bumpers could also be used for spacesuits, although the suits would have to be made in a way that would not limit the astronaut's movement.

Burt Cour-Palais and other research scientists at JSC test various devices in order to find the safest and most practical means of protection.

Cour-Palais's office, for example, is strewn with sheets of aluminum scarred by gaping holes that look like shotgun blasts. These holes, however, are the result of collisions with tiny particles. The particles range in size from infinitesimal—so small the human eye cannot see them—to three-eighths of an inch in diameter. They're fired from hypervelocity (high-speed) light-gas guns at JSC, Marshall Space Flight Center, and Ames Research Center.

The relative speeds and masses of the objects colliding determine the amount of damage, as happened with the paint flake and the space shuttle window.

"If we're going to have human beings in space for long periods of time," added Cour-Palais, "we need to understand orbital debris and make sure that we provide adequate protection against it."

Orbiting trash can

Short-term space trips are not as much of a worry for debris specialists as the long-term space stations of the next decade. These three-hundred-foot-long spacecraft would be an ongoing target for many kinds of orbiting debris.

According to a report in *Space World* magazine, one safeguard being considered for future space stations is a satellite that would hover above a station like a watchdog, and warn of approaching debris.

A proposed orbiting trash collector reaches out and grabs space debris. The robot-like collector would be about 20 feet long and 14 feet in diameter.

A few scientists have suggested some unique ways to help clear away the clutter *before* a space station is launched. Marshall H. Kaplan, head of Spacetech, an aerospace consulting company, has proposed "an orbiting trash can with robot arms that would pick up old satellites and large chunks of debris."

A shuttle would carry the giant garbage collector (about twenty feet long and fourteen feet in diameter) into space and place it in orbit, then return it to earth after it made its rounds. While in orbit, the trash can would be maneuvered from the ground.

"Large oversized pieces of refuse could be fitted with small rocket packs by the robot arms on the trash collector," suggests Kaplan. "The rockets would either steer them to a less menacing orbit or drop them into the atmosphere, where they would burn up."

Cleaning up the cosmos

For little pieces of litter, Robert K. Soberman, director of the applied sciences department at the Franklin Research Center in Philadelphia, has another idea. He suggests a huge orbiting sphere of plastic foam bubbles that would handle both large and small objects.

According to Soberman's plan, the material for the sphere would be carried into space in a canister (metal container) aboard a space

THE FAR SIDE   **BY GARY LARSON**

shuttle. The canister would be activated when it reached an orbit filled with debris. Then it would spray out enough plastic foam to form a translucent sphere measuring about five hundred feet in diameter.

As the waste material bumped into the sphere it would either be swallowed up, or if it passed through, it would be angled over to a less dangerous orbit. "Eventually, the sphere would reenter the atmosphere and burn up with the accumulated debris," reported Soberman. Another possible solution is a laser beam that could vaporize the debris—turn it into steam—or turn it off course.

Many ideas have been suggested and studied, but according to Kessler, NASA officials are not yet ready to choose a solution. "We need to determine more accurately just how many of the smaller objects are whizzing around in space and in which orbits."

Space scientists do agree on one important thing, however. The way to stop collisions from reaching truly dangerous levels is to develop practices that will keep more space debris from forming.

But before this can occur, they need to observe and better understand the nature of space debris. To assist with this research, NASA is using two thirty-one-inch telescopes with remote sensing devices at Lincoln Laboratory in Socorro, New Mexico, to track and record objects as small as marbles. To get an even closer look, they plan to launch a satellite with an eight-inch telescope that could spot debris as small as buckshot.

As scientists continue their research on extraterrestrial trash, the United States Department of State has also taken action. A committee of officials from several government agencies has been established to study the need for a government policy on space debris.

For Kessler, the most urgent need in the area of policy-making is for everyone in the spacecraft community to agree on the importance of keeping spacecraft intact (in one piece) until reentry.

Both Kessler and Joe Loftus, JSC's Assistant Director for Plans, also stress the importance of international cooperation. "It doesn't do any good for one nation to start being a good guy unless everybody

U.S. and Canadian officers examine space debris that fell to earth. Most falling debris burns up entering earth's atmosphere.

starts,'' says Loftus. All spacefaring nations need to agree that space debris is everyone's problem, not just that of one or two superpowers.

What goes up might come down

Since the Space Age began in 1957, more than half of the 10,500 objects launched into orbit have returned to earth. Space professionals claim that most objects that drop out of orbit burn up in the atmosphere surrounding earth, appearing as fiery streaks across the sky. Others vaporize and vanish as they fall. But some objects have actually dropped into backyards and onto highways with a thud!

In 1961, a forty-pound chunk of a United States space probe landed in Cuba, killing a cow. In 1969, debris from *Apollo 11*'s Saturn booster plunked down on the deck of a German ship.

Part of a Soviet gas bottle was recovered in New Zealand, and Soviet metal spheres were found in Spain.

In 1970, one falling object actually stampeded a herd of Texas cattle as it scattered hot metal over Texas, Oklahoma, and Kansas.

Even more startling was a 21-pound cylindrical chunk of metal from *Sputnik IV* that came to rest on a street corner in Manitowoc, Wisconsin.

In Winterhaven, Florida, in 1984, a collection of unidentified scraps impacted a state highway. And in the vicinity of Lowell and Marietta, Ohio, twenty-pound metal spheres crashed to the earth.

Most of the fallen items, like many still in orbit, are not satellites at all, but simply discarded items from space missions. They include plastic containers of human waste and other assorted garbage such as nuts and bolts and booster rocket shells. One report states that a perfectly good Hasselblad camera is still up there somewhere, possibly misplaced by an American astronaut while he was out for a spacewalk.

Analysts at NORAD estimate that by the fall of 1997 the number of *trackable* discarded objects still orbiting in space will reach 19,661. There is apparently no official number of objects that have fallen out of orbit and crashed to earth.

No place on earth is completely safe from space trash. Parts of launch vehicle tanks and shells reportedly have been seen in Africa, Australia, South America, Spain, and Scandinavia.

A universal threat

Scientists at the Johnson Space Center are among the world's foremost experts on the subject of space debris, and yet even they admit there is still much to learn. For years space scientists have had an excellent working knowledge of natural meteoroids, says Joe Loftus, but they are only beginning to understand man-made orbital debris.

For the past twelve years these scientists have been conducting experiments to help them increase this knowledge. They examine satellites and spacecraft parts, like the thermal panel from the *Solar Max*, that are returned from space. They also observe the characteristics of orbiting debris by means of high-powered sensing devices and computer models.

Scientists will use this knowledge to make computer models that will one day enable them to successfully predict collisions and to build effective warning systems and protective equipment.

"We are embarking on a series of studies to find out what various protective and preventive measures cost," said Loftus. "But we don't have the answer to that yet."

Meanwhile, extraterrestrial trash seems to be mounting faster than the means to control it or dispose of it. Researchers warn that orbital debris is a growing hazard to space vehicles. It also has far-reaching effects on launch vehicles, payload (a spacecraft's cargo) design, future space stations, the selection of orbits, and international relations.

Today there are nearly four million pounds of man-made material in earth orbit. At the current rate of space travel, 1.8 million additional pounds of debris will be in orbit each year. By the year 2000 this amount is expected to increase yearly by nearly 2.7 million pounds.

These sobering numbers make it clear that, as human beings increase their time and activity in space, they take with them one of their most serious and threatening problems—pollution.

CHAPTER FIVE

From Trash to Cash— and Other Solutions to Waste Pollution

The problem of waste pollution is serious. But it is not hopeless. "People are not powerless in the face of these complex problems," writes Cynthia Pollock in her booklet, *Mining Urban Wastes: The Potential for Recycling*, published by Worldwatch Institute. "By reducing the amount of waste they produce, and recycling a large share of their discards, individuals can become part of the solution."

In many parts of the country, that is exactly the case. Citizens in cities and towns across the United States are discovering that used clothes are more than rags. And one trip through the typewriter or bottling plant need not reduce paper and glass to rubbish. And food packaging materials can be recycled in one's own kitchen.

An uphill climb

Dan Knapp and Mary Lou Deventer are two people active in demonstrating these ideas. They now travel around the country presenting slide shows about the model recycling system they started in Berkeley, California. Their accomplishments are similar to those of residents of other cities across the United States who have begun converting wastes into resources.

In the winter 1986 issue of *Whole Earth Review*, Dan and Mary Lou shared their story and photos. In 1980, Dan started a recycling company in Berkeley, called Urban Ore. At the beginning, all Dan had was the garbage and trash that had been dumped into an *open* plot of land. "Conditions were unbelievably primitive when we started," said Dan. He had no money to invest in the business.

"To create a work space, I had to move a massive, rat-infested pile of tires." To recover items of value, workers had to convince drivers to drop off their recyclable materials before dumping. But more often, Dan admitted, he and others had to climb the mountain of trash and pull out reusable items by brute force.

"We worked against time and gravity, salvaging what we could under a cascade of garbage," said Dan. Workers spotted valuable items every day, but they couldn't get to them fast enough. So at first they concentrated on gathering only those things that could be sold immediately, such as scrap metal and small reusable household goods.

Turnaround

Hard work and persistence paid off. Business grew so quickly that Dan and Mary Lou soon opened two other locations. In 1985, just five years after their first trip to the dump, Urban Ore's three locations had taken in over six hundred thousand dollars from the sale of reusable items.

Dan claims that virtually anything created by humans will eventually show up at a landfill—doors, tires, toilets, tubs, sinks, lighting fixtures, furniture, and appliances. Dan and others decided to clean up these reusable items, move them to a more desirable location, and then put them up for sale.

Dan also found that cleaning up and repairing useful equipment such as a gas-powered lawn mower could yield a higher price than simply selling it as scrap metal. You can toss it into a mixed metal bin and get less than one dollar for it, explained Dan. But if you

Used sinks, toilets, and bathtubs fill a salvage yard at Urban Ore recycling company in Berkeley, California. Such recycled items are available to buyers at low prices. Urban Ore is one of many recycling companies springing up across America.

have a reuse sales area, it pays to see if the motor runs. "If it runs, somebody will buy it. It should be worth five dollars and it may be worth up to twenty-five dollars," he added.

This principle works with other reusable materials, as well. Nearly anything can be resold. Dan even got a good price for the resale of live plants that had been left for the compost heap (decaying refuse).

Frequently the same construction crews who had dumped the materials in the first place became their best customers. They often purchased parts and materials for use in restoring and constructing homes and office buildings. As a result, materials that would have eventually been buried in a landfill were recycled for the benefit of everyone.

Two other recycling businesses in Berkeley also started small. These specialized in handling the more traditional recyclable items such as cans, bottles, cardboard, and paper. Income from these items now exceeds one million dollars a year.

Another successful recycling area in Berkeley is the *door department* where a wide range of doors are cleaned up, then neatly arranged by size and category. Customers line up to purchase single doors, entry doors, panel doors, solid doors, and hollow core doors— all kinds of doors! Used windows are handled in a similar way.

The building materials recycling facility alone occupies nearly an acre of commercial property and brings in more than two hundred thousand dollars each year.

Between 1982 and the present, Berkeley's refuse transfer station (where garbage is transferred to large trucks and hauled to a landfill forty-five miles away) has changed dramatically. It is now a refuse and recycling transfer station. Recycling occurs *before* refuse is turned into garbage. People who want to recycle can do so conveniently. Dropping off reusable items first reduces the weight of their trash and lowers their dumping fee.

"To dispose of the refuse we make, without making garbage, requires an organizing intelligence," says Dan. "The *Oxford Dictionary of the English Language*—a copy of which I appropriately found in the garbage—lists 'orderly placement' as one of the definitions of the word 'disposal.'"

Used doors are displayed at Urban Ore recycling center. Urban Ore buys items from homeowners or contractors then sells the items to other people.

American dictionaries, on the other hand, tend to associate the word *disposal* with garbage. The true meaning of the word has been lost except in specific situations such as "disposal of a relative's estate."

If a relative of yours died and you were the one to dispose of his belongings, you probably "wouldn't dig a hole and bury everything," said Dan. "Nor would you pile it up and burn it. You would catalogue, separate, and give it away piece by piece. This kind of disposal is truly orderly placement," he added. "Garbage disposal has had its day; recycling disposal is on its way."

Civic pride

As mentioned in the introduction, Cobb County, Georgia, is another area where people have worked together to restore order and beauty to their communities. The Cobb Clean Commission, a volunteer litter organization associated with the national program called Keep America Beautiful, formed a partnership between the county's Solid Waste Department and the Corrections Department.

When the cleanup program began in 1985, the commission did not have volunteers to do the actual cleanup work, so officials went to the Corrections Department. Prisoners were given an opportunity to participate in the program as an alternative to jail.

These volunteers worked under the guidance of the Solid Waste Department. Teams of workers searched through mounds of trash that had been dumped illegally for clues that would indicate where it came from. Owners were tracked down through their own discarded mail, check stubs, or envelopes with return addresses. Then they were notified of the county's ordinances and fined if they failed to comply.

This program worked so successfully that Cobb County reduced its litter by 69 percent in just eighteen months. And the cost of the program was minimal. Uniforms, safety equipment for the participants, and trash bags were the county's only expenses.

"The goal of this program is to keep Cobb clean, reduce litter, and increase community awareness about who is responsible for the litter," said Bob McIntyre, director of the Cobb Solid Waste Department.

The Cobb Clean Commission and the Solid Waste Department have also prepared a special program to educate elementary school children about the problems of waste management.

Now that homeowners and young people know what's going on, many are taking an active part in keeping their communities beautiful. "They are out there cleaning not just complaining," said McIntyre.

Coastal cleanup

In still another part of the country, residents were given an opportunity to participate in a program to clean up their beaches. In 1986 the Center for Environmental Education (CEE) organized a Texas

Citizens all over the country are becoming aware of the need for cleaning up the coast line. Here, citizens participate in a beach cleanup project.

Coastal Cleanup campaign. CEE officials hoped to educate the public about the problems caused by marine debris, and to collect information about the kinds and quantities of trash found on the Texas coastline.

Approximately 2,800 volunteers, including school-age children, participated in the cleanup at twelve coastal sites. Workers filled 7,900 trash bags with nearly 124 tons of debris over a distance of 122 miles.

The most common items found were plastic bottles. Volunteers collected 16,572 of this one item alone! Plastic bags were next, plastic caps and lids third, and metal beverage cans and glass bottles ranked fourth and fifth.

After the cleanup campaign was over, volunteers were hot and tired, but very proud of their work. The beaches were cleaner and residents were more aware of the problem of plastic debris. One zone captain said the experience had changed her life. She offered to help with follow-up activities. Many others also volunteered to work in future cleanup campaigns.

An outstanding result of this campaign is a program called Adopt-a-Beach. The purpose of the program is to encourage Texans to care for a particular section of beach. The goal of the program is to help protect the beauty of the coastline, and to increase the public's awareness of marine debris and beach litter so these problems can be confronted and dealt with.

Recycling ethic

In San Diego, California, city and county officials are at work developing a Master Recycling Plan which will involve the help and cooperation of all residents. Currently, San Diegans are recycling less than 10 percent of their waste. The goal is to raise that to 25 percent by the early 1990s.

For this plan to succeed, however, city and county officials agree that *everyone* will have to get involved. ''We will depend on concerned citizens encouraging their fellow citizens to participate,'' says Councilwoman Judy McCarty.

It will require a new way of thinking—a "recycling ethic," as some call it—about trash disposal. No longer will residents simply bag their trash once a week and set it out on the curb.

The new Master Recycling Plan will require home and business owners to separate the reusable items—glass, cardboard, paper, metal, and aluminum—from the nonreusable. It will mean that every person will be expected to do his or her part to protect the environment and keep the city clean.

Recycling was popular in San Diego, as it was in most parts of the United States, during World War II. In fact, the United States was the world's leader in recycling up until 1945.

After the war, however, citizens changed the way they handled solid wastes. The military no longer needed recyclable items, so people stopped saving them. Garbage disposal also became more

Citizens donate recyclable aluminum to help the war effort. The aluminum was made into weapons during World War II.

sophisticated. New, large trucks pulled up to homes and hauled away trash to large landfills, where it was buried. People gave less and less thought to the waste they created.

But now, forty years later, San Diego and most other cities across the United States face a waste disposal crisis. There simply isn't enough land to handle the 220 million tons of waste produced in the U.S. each year.

Recycling is clearly one of the ways in which citizens can prevent more of our precious land from being set aside for garbage. Recycling will also help to conserve nature's valuable resources.

Coy Smith, San Diego City's Recycling Coordinator, says, "We want to provide the opportunity for everyone to recycle in the most convenient manner possible."

The only requirement the city will make, claims Smith, is that people separate recyclables from the rest of their trash. "Once they do that, they have the option of putting materials on the curb for the city to pick up, giving the recyclables to their favorite charity, or taking them to a recycling center for money."

This city by the bay has also established a new telephone information service called "Litter Line." Office manager Polly Frein says the purpose of the phone line is to help residents identify community litter concerns, report litter-law violations, and draw attention to the need to make San Diego communities cleaner and more beautiful.

Residents can use the line to report illegal dumping and abandoned vehicles, as well as to discuss property maintenance and the proper handling of household and hazardous wastes. Litter Line is an associate of Keep America Beautiful and is funded by a special grant from the County of San Diego.

Nationwide alert

California is just one of many states to step up recycling programs. Oregon requires that cities with more than four thousand residents provide a curbside pick-up service for reusable items. New Jersey is setting up residential recycling programs for three kinds of reusable trash. Rhode Island is providing each homeowner with a bin for plastic bottles, metal, and glass. Newspapers are to be stacked on top. In this no-nonsense program, no exceptions are made. If it's not sorted, it won't be collected!

But even if more states toughen up their disposal laws, recycling alone, according to some experts, won't solve the crisis. Trish L. Ferrand, chairperson for the Coalition for Recyclable Waste, claims the answers ultimately lie with manufacturers. Ferrand and representatives from other environmental groups want manufacturers to think about the disposal problem when they develop new products and packages.

"We want them to acknowledge the full loop," Ferrand told reporters for *Business Week*. Industry can make less waste, she says, by designing products that are reusable.

Steven Lang, associate editor of *Waste-To-Energy Report*, claims that waste problems have received so much attention, people may be slow to recognize some of the technological improvements that are being made. According to a report in *Business Week*, these improvements are significant.

New waste-to-energy plants are protected with rust-resistant ceramics. Redesigned grate systems insure more complete burning. And some of the equipment in modern plants even sorts the trash before incineration, then converts it into what is called refuse-derived fuel—energy that results from the burning of refuse. Many such plants are operating trouble-free today.

In Baltimore, Maryland, a 250-million-dollar incinerator burns up to 2,250 tons of trash each day. And the steam it produces helps heat five hundred city buildings and generates electricity that is sold to Baltimore Gas & Electric Company.

In some eastern states, similar plants will be able to dispose of up to two-thirds of the region's garbage. Connecticut, Delaware, and New Hampshire will each be able to process more than half their waste.

By the year 2000, as much as 40 percent of the nation's garbage could be disposed of in these waste-to-energy plants. Barry A. Mannis of Shearson Lehman Brothers estimates that the waste management industry could bring in as much as eighteen billion dollars a year by the mid-1990s, an increase of eight billion dollars over the current total.

CHAPTER SIX

What YOU Can Do

The garbage glut will not go away. Waste is a necessary by-product of living on planet earth. But it does not have to overpower us. *Education* and *participation* are two of the most important ingredients necessary for changing the way people think about and deal with the problem of waste pollution.

People can learn. And people can participate. No one is too young or too old to take part in some way.

Get involved

The way you use food, energy, water, air, and other natural resources will change your environment in some way. Everyone makes a difference, whether he or she thinks about it or not.

Here are some suggestions based on information published by the Environmental Protection Agency and other concerned groups to help you, your family, and friends contribute to a wholesome and clean environment.

Protect the Water

—Make a list of ways you can save water. Suggest them to your family and friends. Some of these ways might include turning off the water while brushing your teeth, taking shorter showers, using less water in the bathtub, washing larger loads of clothes in order to conserve water, and buying water-saving devices for your toilets.

—Make an exhibit for your school or library showing how drinking water is distributed and wastewater is treated in your community.

—Ask your parents, teacher, scout leader, or other adult leader to take you (and your family, class, or troop) for a visit to a water treatment plant in your community. Then write a report on what you learned and share it with your classmates and family.

Protect the Air

—Cut down on car trips. Even with pollution control devices, cars still emit pollutants. Walk, hike, ride your bike, or take a bus instead of driving. You might also help to organize carpools for group activities.

—Conduct an experiment to find out how dirty the air is in your neighborhood. Smear two sheets of paper on one side with petroleum jelly. Place the sheets next to each other, smeared sides up, on a windowsill. Clamp them in place with the closed window or tape them to the outside of the window. Take one sheet in at the end of the first day and compare it to a clean sheet of paper. Save the dirty sheet. Take the other sheet in after a week. Compare it to the first dirty sheet and to the clean sheet to get some idea of how dirty the air is.

—Choose plastic and pump sprays over aerosol sprays.

Protect the Land

—Sell, trade, or donate used furniture, clothing, appliances, toys, games, books, and other household items.

—Organize a recycling club or campaign in your classroom or neighborhood. Here are some titles you might use: ''Dump It, Don't Drop It,'' ''Beautify Our Neighborhood,'' ''Clean Up Our School.'' Gather newspapers, aluminum cans, glass bottles, and cardboard and sell them to companies that will recycle them.

—Find out which products are biodegradable and choose them over nonbiodegradable items.

—Encourage people you know to avoid littering.

—With an adult leader, organize a field trip to a sanitary landfill or waste-to-energy plant and learn how waste is treated and disposed of.

A once-beautiful woodland pool is littered with debris. Water pollution not only detracts from the beauty of nature but also kills crops.

Protect Yourself from Pesticides

—Learn to recognize pesticides (poisonous chemicals used to destroy pests) by the label on the container. Avoid touching or using pesticide containers, whether full or empty. If you or someone else is contaminated accidentally, get immediate help from an adult. Follow the directions on the container label about what to do in the event of poisoning.

—Adopt a tree or start a small garden. Cut back the weeds around the tree or garden plants to remove hiding places for pests. Water your tree or plants in dry weather to keep them strong and resistant to pests.

—Try to keep your garden pest-free without pesticides. Wear gloves and pick off larger pests like caterpillars and Japanese beetles with your hands. Rid plants of smaller pests by washing them off with a hose.

—Do not harm ladybugs, praying mantises, spiders, toads, and birds. They help control insect pests.

—Wash fruits and vegetables well before eating them.

Protect Yourself from Toxic Substances

—Memorize the "hit list" of toxic chemicals, and stay away from them. Dioxin, polychlorinated biphenyls (PCBs), ethylene dibromide (EDB), and asbestos are among the most deadly.

Dioxin is a waste by-product from the manufacture of herbicides used to kill weeds. Scientists have more to learn about the effects of dioxin, but they already know that it can cause cancer in test animals and skin disease in people. Dioxin can be destroyed by burning.

PCBs are heat-resistant toxic chemicals once used in certain kinds of electrical equipment. PCBs may cause cancer and birth defects in animals. The United States now bans the production of PCBs.

EDB is a pesticide that has caused cancer and birth defects in test animals. Use of EDB on grain, fruit, and soil has been banned in the United States.

Asbestos is a substance composed of natural minerals (silicates) that separate into thin, strong fibers. It is heat and chemical resistant. Asbestos was once sprayed on ceilings to make them fireproof and was also used in a wide variety of other products. When broken down into dust, asbestos can be breathed in, and can cause cancer and lung disease.

Good garbage

Talk with your family about ways to use and reuse "good garbage."

—Switch from paper to cloth napkins. You can even make your own from scraps available at a fabric store.

Workers wear protective clothing to remove asbestos from a public building. Asbestos, a toxic chemical, has been linked with cancer and lung disease. It was once sprayed on ceilings to make them fireproof.

—Use cloth towels and cleaning rags instead of paper towels. Old sheets, T-shirts, and cloth diapers are ideal for this purpose.

—Use old newspaper to clean windows.

—Reuse food packaging materials such as plastic and glass containers from margarine, juice, jam, sauces, soups, and other foods.

—Use the other side of used notepaper, stationery, computer paper, or other writing paper for notes, memos, first drafts of homework.

—Save plastic food bags and other plastic wrap such as that used on dry cleaning. Reuse these items for storing leftover food, wrapping sandwiches, holding soiled clothes or used cleaning rags, or to temporarily store clothing that needs to be repaired or ironed. *Be sure to store unused plastic wrap out of the reach of small children.*

—Set aside a shelf, a large box, or even a closet to store used shoestrings, fabric and paper scraps, ribbons, yarn, magazines, buttons, small plastic containers and cups, and other reusable items. Use them to create homemade gifts, art and craft activities, gift wrap, and other projects.

Philadelphia residents add their bundles to the growing pile of trash along a city street. Striking trash collectors left Philadelphia without services for over a week.

—Share items you don't want or need with people and organizations that can use them. Children's hospitals, homes for the aged, nursery schools, classrooms, centers for the homeless, and organizations for the handicapped welcome donations of this kind.

Spread the word

The subject of waste pollution is so complex that you and other students may feel there is little you can do to make a *major* difference. But that's not true.

Michaela Spehn, a fourteen-year-old student at Bell Junior High School in San Diego, entered her essay on waste pollution in the 1988 writing competition sponsored by the *San Diego Union* and *Tribune* and the *Greater San Diego Reading Association*. Her essay, which won first place, was chosen from two thousand entries submitted by area students to the contest held in conjunction with *National Newspaper Week*. (Reprinted below with permission of the *San Diego Union*.)

TRASH CRUSH

Modern society has a major problem with where to put its waste. The average citizen of the United States produces about four to six pounds of rubbish every day, a staggering amount compared to most countries.

The Quality of Life Board released a comprehensive report on San Diego's trash problem and possible solutions. Although the City Council requested the report, the mayor refused to facilitate its presentation before the council prior to the November election when the Clean Air Initiative was passed.

The Clean Air Initiative bars any trash-to-energy plant that burns more than 500 tons of trash per day from: increasing toxic pollutants within the city; being built within a three-mile radius of a hospital, child-care facility, nursing home, or elementary school; or making demands on the city's treated water-distribution system. The initiative could just as well have said that no plants burning more than 500 tons a day could be built, since the siting restrictions alone rule out virtually all locations within the city. This means that the most promising way to handle trash is now lost to San Diego.

San Diego is no longer a small town. Every two weeks, San Diegans produce enough waste to fill Jack Murphy Stadium to the top row of seats. If a safe and environmentally sound way to handle this solid waste is not found soon, in 11 years San Diego will run out of landfill space. What will we do with our trash then?

If we want to preserve our planet—as well as the life we share with all living creatures—each one of us must do what we can to keep our environment wholesome and clean for ourselves and for the generations to follow.

You may not wish to write or speak out publicly on the subject of waste pollution, but you can make a difference nonetheless. Continue to learn as much as you can and use good waste management practices. Read some of the books and write to some of the organizations listed in the back of this book.

Share what you learn with family and friends. Get involved in a community or beach cleanup and beautification program, or volunteer your time at a recycling center.

Glossary

biodegradable: Able to be broken down into simple, natural products or decomposed by animals, fungi, and microscopic plants called bacteria.

by-product: Something that is produced as a result of making the main product. A *waste by-product* is an unwanted by-product that can either be disposed of or recycled.

compost: Decayed refuse.

contamination: An impurity; a pollutant.

debris: Scattered fragments; litter; rubbish.

decompose: To break down and change in both chemistry and appearance through bacterial action.

dioxin: A powerful poison used in certain weed-killing compounds that has been found to have strong, harmful effects on humans.

dispose: To get rid of something.

dump: A place for throwing trash or garbage.

entangled: Snared; unable to get out of or through.

environment: All of the surrounding objects, conditions, and influences that affect living things.

environmental pollution: Waste products that contaminate the environment.

extraterrestrial: Outside of the earth and its atmosphere.

fallout: The radioactive particles or dust that falls to earth following a nuclear explosion.

garbage: Any kind of waste matter.

hazardous waste: Waste matter that is dangerous to health or environment.

incinerator: A furnace for burning trash or solid waste to ashes.

landfill: A place where garbage or trash is deposited and covered with earth. A common system of trash disposal.

litter: Little bits of trash and debris left scattered about.

methane: A colorless, odorless, flammable gas formed naturally from the decomposition of plants or other organic matter.

natural resources: Materials supplied by nature, such as minerals, timber, water, and land, that are useful and necessary for life.

particle: A very tiny amount of something. Any of the extremely small units that make up matter.

pesticide: Any one of various substances used to kill harmful insects, fungi, vermin, or other living organisms that prey on plant life or in some other way are harmful.

pollutant: Waste product that contaminates the environment.

radiation sickness: A disease or unhealthy condition resulting from overexposure to radiation from radioactive materials.

recycle: To go through a cycle again; to reuse; to put wastes, rubbish, or trash through a purifying process and convert it to useful products.

refuse: Unwanted material; trash.

resources: Air, water, soil, trees, plants, minerals, wildlife, and other things that make up the natural wealth of the earth.

rubbish: Waste; trash; garbage.

salvage: Saved goods.

sanitation: Waste disposal practices that preserve health and safety.

seep: To leak slowly, as a liquid, through a loose substance such as soil.

sewage: Waste matter carried off in sewers and drains.

space junk: Space litter or debris; refers specifically to pieces of abandoned or exploded equipment such as rockets, satellites, nose cones, and other spacecraft parts left in orbit.

toxic waste: Waste from poisonous or hazardous chemicals.

trash: Worthless material; litter; rubbish.

waste: Material that is useless; garbage; trash; litter.

waste disposal: Methods for disposing of, or getting rid of, waste.

waste disposal management: Systems for managing the safe disposal of waste.

Organizations To Contact

The following organizations are concerned with the issues covered in this book. All of them have publications or information available for interested readers. The descriptions are derived from materials provided by the organizations themselves.

Center for Environmental Education
National Office
1725 DeSales St. NW
Washington, DC 20036
(202) 737-3600

The Center for Environmental Education, a marine conservation organization, works to protect whales, seals, sea turtles, and other endangered sea creatures from extinction.

Center for Environmental Information
33 S. Washington St.
Rochester, NY 14608
(716) 546-3796

The Center for Environmental Information is an organization which, through publications, educational programs, conferences, and its library, provides information about environmental issues.

The Conservation Foundation
1255 Twenty-third St. NW
Washington, DC 20037
(202) 293-4800

The Conservation Foundation is an organization that conducts research on environmental and resource management. It is dedicated to improving the quality of the environment and to promoting wise use of the earth's resources.

Lawrence Hall of Science
University of California
Berkeley, CA 94620
(415) 642-5132

The Lawrence Hall of Science is a place where everyone can enjoy the excitement of exploring science. It is a resource for schools, a public science center for visitors, and a research unit of the University of California. All of the hall's activities directly involve participants in the discovery process.

National Aeronautics and Space Administration
Lyndon B. Johnson Space Center
Houston, TX 77058
(713) 483-5111 (Public Affairs Office)

The National Aeronautics and Space Administration conducts and coordinates United States nonmilitary flight research within and beyond the earth's atmosphere. Research into space debris is conducted at the Johnson Space Center in Houston, Texas, one of NASA's research sites.

The Nuclear Information and Resource Service
1616 P St. NW
Washington, DC 20036
(202) 328-0002

The Nuclear Information and Resource Service is a national organization working solely on nuclear power concerns. It provides citizens and the media with information about nuclear issues.

Sierra Club
730 Polk St.
San Francisco, CA 94109
(415) 776-2211

The Sierra Club has been working to protect and conserve the natural resources of the Sierra Nevada, the United States, and the world since 1892.

U.S. Environmental Protection Agency
Office of Public Affairs (A-107)
Washington, DC 20460

The U.S. Environmental Protection Agency is an agency of the United States government responsible for implementing federal laws designed to protect the environment. This organization deals with questions, issues, and decisions concerning air, water, and land.

Worldwatch Institute
1776 Massachusetts Ave. NW
Washington, DC 20036
(202) 452-1999

Worldwatch Institute is an independent, nonprofit research organization created to analyze and to focus attention on global problems. Publications are written for a worldwide audience of decision makers, scholars, and the general public.

Suggestions for Further Reading

Hodges, Laurent, *Environmental Pollution*. Orlando, FL: Holt, Rinehart & Winston, 1977.

Kiefer, Irene, *Poisoned Land: The Problems of Hazardous Waste*. New York: Atheneum Children's Books (Macmillan), 1981.

King, Jonathan, *Troubled Water*. Emmaus, PA: Rodale Press, 1985.

Luoma, Jon, *Troubled Skies, Troubled Waters*. New York: Penguin, 1985.

Magnuson, Ed, "A Problem That Cannot Be Buried: The Poisoning of America Continues." *Time*. Oct. 14, 1985, 76-84.

Morganthau, Tom, "Don't Go Near the Water." *Newsweek*. 112 (Aug. 1, 1988), 44-50.

Special issue: "Can Man Save This Fragile Earth?" *National Geographic*, 174 (Dec. 1988), 765-945.

Pringle, Laurence, *Throwing Things Away*. Cincinnati: Crowell, 1986.

Thackray, Sue, *Looking at Pollution*. North Pomfret, VT: David and Charles, 1987.

Timberlake, Lloyd, *Only One Earth*. New York: Sterling, 1987.

Woods, Geraldine and Harold, *Pollution*. New York: Franklin Watts, 1985.

Index

Acknowledgments

The author wishes to thank all of the individuals and organizations whose expertise and photographs contributed to the writing of this book.

California Waste Management Board

Center for Environmental Education, Kathy O'Hara

Center for Marine Conservation

Coastal Zone Management, Dee Garner, Editor

Environmental Protection Agency, Darci Dudel

National Aeronautics and Space Administration, Donald J. Kessler
and Kelly Humphries

National Oceanic and Atmospheric Administration

San Diego Litter Line, Polly Frein

Worldwatch Institute

Picture Credits

About the Author

Karen O'Connor is an award-winning author. She has over 300 magazine articles, two films, and twenty published books to her credit, including *Contributions of Women: Literature, Maybe You Belong in a Zoo,* and the best-selling *Sally Ride and the New Astronauts.*

She is an instructor for The Institute of Children's Literature and teaches writing workshops for the University of California and other adult education programs in the state. She has served as a national language arts consultant for the Glencoe Publishing Company and is a frequent guest speaker at schools and professional groups throughout the country.

EDUCATION